Contents

21st Century – page 2
Transfers I – page 6
First Goals I – page 9
Red Cards – page 11
Memorable Goals – page 13
Memorable Games – page 15
Transfers II – page 17
Cup Games – page 20
First Goals II – page 23
European Games – page 25

21st Century answers – page 28
Transfers I answers – page 33
First Goals I answers – page 37
Red Cards answers – page 39
Memorable Goals answers – page 42
Memorable Games answers – page 45
Transfers II answers – page 48
Cup Games answers – page 53
First Goals II answers – page 56
European Games answers – page 58

21st Century

1) Who was Everton manager at the beginning of the 21st Century?

2) Tottenham's Son Heung-Min was sent off against Everton in 2019 for a challenge which resulted in which player suffering an horrendous ankle injury?

3) Jordan Pickford made penalty saves in consecutive Premier League games in October 2018, which two players did he deny from the spot?

4) Which Newcastle United player scored twice in injury time to secure a 2-2 in the meeting between the two sides in January 2020?

5) Who became the youngest ever Premier League scorer when he netted against Crystal Palace aged 16 years, 8 months and 27 days in April 2005?

6) Who became the youngest player to appear for Everton when he debuted against Blackburn Rovers in the Premier League in 2008 aged 16 years, 6 months and 9 days?

7) Who did Everton face in Tony Hibbert's testimonial match?

8) Which player scored an own goal in the 2-1 defeat away at Newcastle in November 2011?

9) In October 2016 goalkeeper Maarten Stekelenburg saved two penalties in a match against which team?

10) Which player was brought on as a substitute against Manchester United in December 2019, only to be taken off again less than twenty minutes later?

11) Arouna Kone hit a hat trick against which team in a 6-2 win in November 2015?

12) Who was the unlikely scorer of a hat-trick in the 4-0 victory over Leeds United in September 2003?

13) Who became the first Costa Rican to appear for the club after signing from Sunderland in 2012?

14) What was the result of Marco Silva's last game in charge of the club?

15) What was the result of Ronald Koeman's last game in charge of the club?

16) What shirt number did Wayne Rooney wear throughout his first spell at Everton?

17) Who did Phil Neville replace as club captain in 2007?

18) In which season did Everton qualify for the Champions League by finishing 4th in the Premier League?

19) Who scored a goal in the first minute of David Moyes' first game in charge against Fulham in March 2002?

20) Duncan Ferguson took over as caretaker manager in December 2019, what was the result in his first game in charge against Chelsea?

21) Who had a late winner controversially ruled out by VAR late on in the 1-1 draw with Manchester United in March 2020?

Transfers I

1) Which Italian defender was bought from Newcastle in July 2000?

2) Which Croatian left the club in March 2000 to join Hajduk Split?

3) Paul Gascoigne arrived after leaving which club in July 2000?

4) Which striker returned to the club from Newcastle in August 2000?

5) From which German club was Thomas Gravesen signed in July 2000?

6) Which England international was sold to Liverpool in July 2000?

7) Alan Stubbs signed on a free from which club in 2001?

8) Which midfielder was bought from Coventry in February 2002?

9) To which club was Abel Xavier sold in 2002?

10) Everton bought which goalkeeper from Arsenal in July 2002?

11) Which Irish player signed from Sunderland in September 2003?

12) Who signed for IFK Gothenburg after leaving Everton in 2004?

13) Club legend Tim Cahill was bought from which English team in 2004?

14) Which future England international signed from Cambridge United in 2005?

15) David Unsworth signed for which club on a free after leaving Everton in 2004?

16) Which club was Thomas Gravesen sold to in 2005?

17) Mikel Arteta arrived at the club in 2005 from which Spanish side?

18) Which defender was bought from Sheffield United in July 2007?

19) Which club did David Weir sign for after leaving Everton in January 2007?

20) Steven Pienaar was purchased from which club in 2007?

21) James McFadden was sold to which club in January 2008?

22) From which Irish side did Everton sign Seamus Coleman in January 2009?

23) Which Russian arrived from Lokomotiv Moscow in August 2009?

First Goals I – Name the clubs that these players scored their first goal for the club against

1) Richarlison

2) Ross Barkley

3) Tom Davies

4) Leighton Baines

5) Phil Jagielka

6) Romelu Lukaku

7) Andrew Johnson

8) Jermaine Beckford

9) Dominic Calvert-Lewin

10) Gylfi Sigurdsson

11) Joleon Lescott

12) Nikica Jelavic

13) Leon Osman

Red Cards

1) Which two Everton players were sent off during the 1-1 draw with Leeds in May 2000?

2) Who was dismissed during the 2-1 loss to Arsenal in August 2003?

3) Richarlison was dismissed against which side in a 2-2 draw in August 2018?

4) Who picked up a red card during the November 2010 encounter with Bolton?

5) James Beattie was given his marching orders against Chelsea in February 2005 after head butting which player?

6) John Ruddy made his only Everton appearance in the 1-0 win over Blackburn in February 2006 after which goalkeeper was sent off early on?

7) Which defender was given a straight red for his challenge on Divock Origi in the April 2016 Merseyside derby?

8) Who was controversially sent off versus Chelsea in the 3-1 loss in December 2002?

9) Who was sent off after picking up two yellow cards against QPR in October 2012?

10) Everton claimed a dramatic 3-2 away win over Watford in February 2020 despite which player being sent off with the score at 2-2?

11) Everton lost the Merseyside derby 2-1 in October 2007, which two Everton players were dismissed?

12) What was unusual about Kurt Zouma's dismissal against Watford in February 2019?

13) Who was dismissed after collecting two yellow cards in the 5-2 loss to Arsenal in October 2017?

Memorable Goals

1) In what year did Wayne Rooney score his stunning first Premier League goal against Arsenal?

2) Leighton Baines scored two free kicks in one game against which team in September 2009?

3) Ross Barkley scored the goal of the month for May 2014 with a superb long-range strike against which team?

4) Who scored a last-minute solo goal to secure a 3-1 win over Manchester United in February 2010?

5) James McFadden scored the goal of the month for April 2007 with his flick and volley versus which side?

6) Tim Howard scored a memorable goal from his own half against Bolton Wanderers in January 2012, but who was in goal for the opposition?

7) Leon Osman hit a superb swerving effort with his left foot past which Manchester City goalkeeper in the March 2013 meeting between the two sides?

8) Who scored a stunning last-minute equaliser to clinch a point at Anfield in September 2014?

9) Kevin Mirallas opening the scoring against which opposition when he cut back and curled a fantastic effort into the far corner in November 2014?

10) Ross Barkley hit a screamer with his left foot to win the goal of the month award against QPR in December of what year?

11) Wayne Rooney scored from inside his own half against which team in November 2017?

12) Leighton Baines hit his powerful long-range free kick past which Newcastle United goalkeeper in January 2013?

Memorable Games

1) Which two players scored in stoppage time to rescue a 3-3 draw against Manchester United in September 2010?

2) Who scored on his Everton debut as Manchester City were hammered 4-0 in January 2017?

3) Everton tore Arsenal apart at Goodison in April 2014, what was the final score?

4) Everton were humiliated at home by Arsenal in August 2009, what was the result?

5) Everton beat West Ham 5-0 in September 2001, which former toffee scored an own goal during the game?

6) Everton won a thriller against Derby County away from home in March 2002, what was the final score?

7) By what score did Everton hammer Sunderland in November 2007?

8) Everton were on the receiving end of a thumping against Arsenal in May 2005, what was the final result?

9) Which Bolton player scored a late own goal to gift Everton a 3-2 win in December 2004?

10) Everton severely dented Manchester United's title hopes by staging a comeback in their April 2012 encounter, what was the final score?

11) How many goals did Romelu Lukaku scored in the 6-3 win over Bournemouth in February 2017?

Transfers II

1) Which central midfielder signed from Manchester United in January 2012?

2) Who was Yakubu sold to in August 2011?

3) Which forward player arrived on a free from Rangers in July 2012?

4) From which club did Everton buy John Stones in January 2013?

5) Who did Tim Cahill sign for after leaving Everton in July 2012?

6) Which three outfield players signed from Wigan Athletic in the summer of 2013?

7) Which goalkeeper was bought from Atletico Madrid in July 2013, having been on loan to Wigan Athletic the previous season?

8) Which striker was sold to West Brom in September 2013?

9) Which two strikers arrived from Chelsea in the summer of 2014?

10) Which midfield player was bought from Manchester United in June 2015?

11) Which England international was bought from Tottenham in September 2015?

12) Which young player arrived from Sheffield United in July 2016?

13) Sylvain Distin signed for which team after leaving the club in July 2015?

14) Tim Howard left Everton in June 2016, signing for which side?

15) Which central defender arrived from Swansea City in August 2016?

16) Ademola Lookman was bought from which club in 2017?

17) Who did Steven Pienaar sign for in August 2016?

18) Which striker was bought from Besiktas in 2018?

19) Who was Gerard Deulofeu sold to in July 2017?

20) Which two players were bought from Barcelona in August 2018?

21) Which player was sold to Werder Bremen in July 2018?

22) Which player was purchased from Mainz in August 2019?

23) Who was transferred to Paris Saint Germain in July 2019?

Cup Games

1) Leicester knocked Everton out of the League Cup in December 2019, but who had scored a dramatic late equaliser for the toffees to take the game to penalties?

2) Everton lost in the 2016 League Cup Semi Final to Manchester City by what aggregate score?

3) Which lower league team beat Everton in the FA Cup Fourth Round in 2001?

4) Everton reached the 2009 FA Cup Final by defeating Manchester United on penalties in the Semi Final, who scored the final penalty in the shoot out?

5) Who scored in the first minute of the 2009 FA Cup final to give Everton the lead before they eventually lost out to Chelsea?

6) Liverpool knocked Everton out of the FA Cup at the Semi Final stage in 2012 after scoring a late winner to secure a 2-1 win, but who had put Everton ahead in the game?

7) Everton were beaten in the 2013 FA Cup Quarter Final by which team, who then went on to lift the cup?

8) Which non-league side did Everton beat 2-0 at home in the 2012 FA Cup Third Round?

9) Everton lost out on penalties after a replay in the 2015 FA Cup Third Round against West Ham, what was the remarkable score in the shoot out?

10) Everton conceded a late goal to lose 2-1 against which side in the 2003 FA Cup Third Round?

11) Everton lost to Liverpool in the FA Cup Third Round of 2020, which Liverpool youngster scored the only goal of the game?

12) Who scored the late winner in extra time to knock Liverpool out of the FA Cup at the Fourth Round stage in 2009?

First Goals II

1) Tim Cahill

2) Seamus Coleman

3) Louis Saha

4) Yannick Bolasie

5) James Beattie

6) Tomasz Radzinski

7) Victor Anichebe

8) Sylvain Distin

9) Yakubu

10) Marouane Fellaini

11) Gerard Deulofeu

12) Lucas Digne

13) Moise Kean

European Games

1) The toffees lost 4-2 on penalties versus Fiorentina at the last 16 stage of the 2007/08 UEFA Cup, which two players missed in the shoot-out?

2) In 2005 Everton lost the first leg of their UEFA Cup First Round tie by what score line against Dinamo Bukarest?

3) Which side did Everton hammer 8-1 on aggregate in the UEFA Cup Third Round in 2008?

4) Everton were knocked out of the UEFA Cup in the First Round by which team in 2008?

5) Everton qualified for the knockout stages of the 2009/10 Europa League by finishing second in the group stage, behind which team?

6) Everton topped the table in their 2014/15 Europa League group by beating Wolfsburg by what score in the final group stage game?

7) Who knocked Everton out of the 2014/15 Europa League at the last 16 stage?

8) Everton managed only one win during their Europa League 2017/18 campaign, beating which team 3-0 away from home?

9) Which referee controversially ruled out a Duncan Ferguson goal to effectively end their hopes of beating Villarreal in the qualifying round of the Champions League in 2005?

10) What was the aggregate score line in that Champions League Qualifying Round tie?

Answers

21st Century Answers

1) Who was Everton manager at the beginning of the 21st Century?
Walter Smith

2) Tottenham's Son Heung-Min was sent off against Everton in 2019 for a challenge which resulted in which player suffering an horrendous ankle injury?
Andre Gomes

3) Jordan Pickford made penalty saves in consecutive Premier League games in October 2018, which two players did he deny from the spot?
Luka Milivojevic and Paul Pogba

4) Which Newcastle United player scored twice in injury time to secure a 2-2 in the meeting between the two sides in January 2020?
Florian Lejeune

5) Who became the youngest ever Premier League scorer when he netted against Crystal Palace aged 16 years, 8 months and 27 days in April 2005?
James Vaughan

6) Who became the youngest player to appear for Everton when he debuted against Blackburn Rovers in the Premier League in 2008 aged 16 years, 6 months and 9 days?
Jose Baxter

7) Who did Everton face in Tony Hibbert's testimonial match?
AEK Athens

8) Which player scored an own goal in the 2-1 defeat away at Newcastle in November 2011?
Johnny Heitinga

9) In October 2016 goalkeeper Maarten Stekelenburg saved two penalties in a match against which team?
Manchester City

10) Which player was brought on as a substitute against Manchester United in December 2019, only to be taken off again less than twenty minutes later?
Moise Kean

11) Arouna Kone hit a hat trick against which team in a 6-2 win in November 2015?
Sunderland

12) Who was the unlikely scorer of a hat-trick in the 4-0 victory over Leeds United in September 2003?
Steve Watson

13) Who became the first Costa Rican to appear for the club after signing from Sunderland in 2012?
Bryan Oviedo

14) What was the result of Marco Silva's last game in charge of the club?
5-2 loss to Liverpool

15) What was the result of Ronald Koeman's last game in charge of the club?
5-2 loss to Arsenal

16) What shirt number did Wayne Rooney wear throughout his first spell at Everton?
18

17) Who did Phil Neville replace as club captain in 2007?
David Weir

18) In which season did Everton qualify for the Champions League by finishing 4th in the Premier League?
2004/05

19) Who scored a goal in the first minute of David Moyes' first game in charge against Fulham in March 2002?
David Unsworth

20) Duncan Ferguson took over as caretaker manager in December 2019, what was the result in his first game in charge against Chelsea?
Everton 3-1 Chelsea

21) Who had a late winner controversially ruled out by VAR late on in the 1-1 draw with Manchester United in March 2020?
Dominic Calvert-Lewin

Transfers I Answers

1) Which Italian defender was bought from Newcastle in July 2000?
   Alessandro Pistone

2) Which Croatian left the club in March 2000 to join Hajduk Split?
   Slaven Bilic

3) Paul Gascoigne arrived after leaving which club in July 2000?
   Middlesbrough

4) Which striker returned to the club from Newcastle in August 2000?
   Duncan Ferguson

5) From which German club was Thomas Gravesen signed in July 2000?
   Hamburg

6) Which England international was sold to Liverpool in July 2000?
   Nick Barmby

7) Alan Stubbs signed on a free from which club in 2001?
Celtic

8) Which midfielder was bought from Coventry in February 2002?
Lee Carsley

9) To which club was Abel Xavier sold in 2002?
Liverpool

10) Everton bought which goalkeeper from Arsenal in July 2002?
Richard Wright

11) Which Irish player signed from Sunderland in September 2003?
Kevin Kilbane

12) Who signed for IFK Gothenburg after leaving Everton in 2004?
Niclas Alexandersson

13) Club legend Tim Cahill was bought from which English team in 2004?
Millwall

14) Which future England international signed from Cambridge United in 2005?
John Ruddy

15) David Unsworth signed for which club on a free after leaving Everton in 2004?
Portsmouth

16) Which club was Thomas Gravesen sold to in 2005?
Real Madrid

17) Mikel Arteta arrived at the club in 2005 from which Spanish side?
Real Sociedad

18) Which defender was bought from Sheffield United in July 2007?
Phil Jaglelka

19) Which club did David Weir sign for after leaving Everton in January 2007?
Rangers

20) Steven Pienaar was purchased from which club in 2007?
Borussia Dortmund

21) James McFadden was sold to which club in January 2008?
Birmingham City

22) From which Irish side did Everton sign Seamus Coleman in January 2009?
Sligo Rovers

23) Which Russian arrived from Lokomotiv Moscow in August 2009?
Diniyar Bilyaletdinov

First Goals I Answers

1) Richarlison
   Wolverhampton Wanderers

2) Ross Barkley
   Norwich City

3) Tom Davies
   Manchester City

4) Leighton Baines
   Portsmouth

5) Phil Jagielka
   AZ Alkmaar

6) Romelu Lukaku
   West Ham

7) Andrew Johnson
   Watford

8) Jermaine Beckford
   Huddersfield Town

9) Dominic Calvert-Lewin
   Hull City

10) Gylfi Sigurdsson
    Hajduk Split

11) Joleon Lescott
    Aston Villa

12) Nikica Jelavic
    Tottenham Hotspur

13) Leon Osman
    Wolverhampton Wanderers

Red Cards Answers

1) Which two Everton players were sent off during the 1-1 draw with Leeds in May 2000?
   Richard Dunne and Don Hutchinson

2) Who was dismissed during the 2-1 loss to Arsenal in August 2003?
   Li Tie

3) Richarlison was dismissed against which side in a 2-2 draw in August 2018?
   Bournemouth

4) Who picked up a red card during the November 2010 encounter with Bolton?
   Marouane Fellaini

5) James Beattie was given his marching orders against Chelsea in February 2005 after head butting which player?
   William Gallas

6) John Ruddy made his only Everton appearance in the 1-0 win over Blackburn in February 2006 after which goalkeeper was sent off early on?
Iain Turner

7) Which defender was given a straight red for his challenge on Divock Origi in the April 2016 Merseyside derby?
Ramiro Funes Mori

8) Who was controversially sent off versus Chelsea in the 3-1 loss in December 2002?
David Unsworth

9) Who was sent off after picking up two yellow cards against QPR in October 2012?
Steven Pienaar

10) Everton claimed a dramatic 3-2 away win over Watford in February 2020 despite which player being sent off with the score at 2-2?
Fabian Delph

11) Everton lost the Merseyside derby 2-1 in October 2007, which two Everton players were dismissed?
Tony Hibbert and Phil Neville

12) What was unusual about Kurt Zouma's dismissal against Watford in February 2019?
It was after the full-time whistle

13) Who was dismissed after collecting two yellow cards in the 5-2 loss to Arsenal in October 2017?
Idrissa Gueye

Memorable Goals Answers

1) In what year did Wayne Rooney score his stunning first Premier League goal against Arsenal?
   2002

2) Leighton Baines scored two free kicks in one game against which team in September 2009?
   West Ham

3) Ross Barkley scored the goal of the month for May 2014 with a superb long-range strike against which team?
   Manchester City

4) Who scored a last-minute solo goal to secure a 3-1 win over Manchester United in February 2010?
   Jack Rodwell

5) James McFadden scored the goal of the month for April 2007 with his flick and volley versus which side?
   Charlton Athletic

6) Tim Howard scored a memorable goal from his own half against Bolton Wanderers in January 2012, but who was in goal for the opposition?
Adam Bogdan

7) Leon Osman hit a superb swerving effort with his left foot past which Manchester City goalkeeper in the March 2013 meeting between the two sides?
Joe Hart

8) Who scored a stunning last-minute equaliser to clinch a point at Anfield in September 2014?
Phil Jagielka

9) Kevin Mirallas opening the scoring against which opposition when he cut back and curled a fantastic effort into the far corner in November 2014?
Tottenham Hotspur

10) Ross Barkley hit a screamer with his left foot to win the goal of the month award against QPR in December of what year?
2014

11) Wayne Rooney scored from inside his own half against which team in November 2017?
West Ham

12) Leighton Baines hit his powerful long-range free kick past which Newcastle United goalkeeper in January 2013?
Tim Krul

Memorable Games Answers

1) Which two players scored in stoppage time to rescue a 3-3 draw against Manchester United in September 2010?
Tim Cahill and Mikel Arteta

2) Who scored on his Everton debut as Manchester City were hammered 4-0 in January 2017?
Ademola Lookman

3) Everton tore Arsenal apart at Goodison in April 2014, what was the final score?
3-0

4) Everton were humiliated at home by Arsenal in August 2009, what was the result?
6-1

5) Everton beat West Ham 5-0 in September 2001, which former toffee scored an own goal during the game?
Don Hutchinson

6) Everton won a thriller against Derby County away from home in March 2002, what was the final score?
4-3

7) By what score did Everton hammer Sunderland in November 2007?
7-1

8) Everton were on the receiving end of a thumping against Arsenal in May 2005, what was the final result?
7-0

9) Which Bolton player scored a late own goal to gift Everton a 3-2 win in December 2004?
Radhi Jaidi

10) Everton severely dented Manchester United's title hopes by staging a comeback in their April 2012 encounter, what was the final score?
4-4

11) How many goals did Romelu Lukaku scored in the 6-3 win over Bournemouth in February 2017?
Four

Transfers II Answers

1) Which central midfielder signed from Manchester United in January 2012?
Darron Gibson

2) Who was Yakubu sold to in August 2011?
Blackburn Rovers

3) Which forward player arrived on a free from Rangers in July 2012?
Steven Naismith

4) From which club did Everton buy John Stones in January 2013?
Barnsley

5) Who did Tim Cahill sign for after leaving Everton in July 2012?
New York Red Bulls

6) Which three outfield players signed from Wigan Athletic in the summer of 2013?
Arouna Kone, Antolin Alcaraz and James McCarthy

7) Which goalkeeper was bought from Atletico Madrid in July 2013, having been on loan to Wigan Athletic the previous season?
Joel Robles

8) Which striker was sold to West Brom in September 2013?
Victor Anichebe

9) Which two strikers arrived from Chelsea in the summer of 2014?
Romelu Lukaku and Samuel Eto'o

10) Which midfield player was bought from Manchester United in June 2015?
Tom Cleverley

11) Which England international was bought from Tottenham in September 2015?
Aaron Lennon

12) Which young player arrived from Sheffield United in July 2016?
Dominic Calvert-Lewin

13) Sylvain Distin signed for which team after leaving the club in July 2015?
Bournemouth

14) Tim Howard left Everton in June 2016, signing for which side?
Colorado Rapids

15) Which central defender arrived from Swansea City in August 2016?
Ashley Williams

16) Ademola Lookman was bought from which club in 2017?
Charlton Athletic

17) Who did Steven Pienaar sign for in August 2016?
Sunderland

18) Which striker was bought from Besiktas in 2018?
Cenk Tosun

19) Who was Gerard Deulofeu sold to in July 2017?
Barcelona

20) Which two players were bought from Barcelona in August 2018?
Lucas Digne and Yerry Mina

21) Which player was sold to Werder Bremen in July 2018?
Davy Klaassen

22) Which player was purchased from Mainz in August 2019?
Jean-Philippe Gbamin

23) Who was transferred to Paris Saint-Germain in July 2019?
Idrissa Gueye

Cup Games Answers

1) Leicester knocked Everton out of the League Cup in December 2019, but who had scored a dramatic late equaliser for the toffees to take the game to penalties?
Leighton Baines

2) Everton lost in the 2016 League Cup Semi Final to Manchester City by what aggregate score?
4-3

3) Which lower league team beat Everton in the FA Cup Fourth Round in 2001?
Tranmere

4) Everton reached the 2009 FA Cup Final by defeating Manchester United on penalties in the Semi Final, who scored the final penalty in the shoot out?
Phil Jagielka

5) Who scored in the first minute of the 2009 FA Cup final to give Everton the lead before they eventually lost out to Chelsea?
Louis Saha

6) Liverpool knocked Everton out of the FA Cup at the Semi Final stage in 2012 after scoring a late winner to secure a 2-1 win, but who had put Everton ahead in the game?
Nikica Jelavic

7) Everton were beaten in the 2013 FA Cup Quarter Final by which team, who then went on to lift the cup?
Wigan Athletic

8) Which non-league side did Everton beat 2-0 at home in the 2012 FA Cup Third Round?
Tamworth

9) Everton lost out on penalties after a replay in the 2015 FA Cup Third Round against West Ham, what was the remarkable score in the shoot out?
11-10

10) Everton conceded a late goal to lose 2-1 against which side in the 2003 FA Cup Third Round?
Shrewsbury

11) Everton lost to Liverpool in the FA Cup Third Round of 2020, which Liverpool youngster scored the only goal of the game?
Curtis Jones

12) Who scored the late winner in extra time to knock Liverpool out of the FA Cup at the Fourth Round stage in 2009?
Dan Gosling

First Goals II Answers

1) Tim Cahill
   Manchester City

2) Seamus Coleman
   Brentford

3) Louis Saha
   Fulham

4) Yannick Bolasie
   Burnley

5) James Beattie
   Sunderland

6) Tomasz Radzinski
   West Ham

7) Victor Anichebe
   West Brom

8) Sylvain Distin
   AEK Athens

9) Yakubu
Bolton Wanderers

10) Marouane Fellaini
Newcastle United

11) Gerard Deuloteu
Stevenage

12) Lucas Digne
Watford

13) Moise Kean
Newcastle United

European Games Answers

1) The toffees lost 4-2 on penalties versus Fiorentina at the last 16 stage of the 2007/08 UEFA Cup, which two players missed in the shoot-out?
Yakubu and Phil Jagielka

2) In 2005 Everton lost the first leg of their UEFA Cup First Round tie by what score line against Dinamo Bukarest?
5-1

3) Which side did Everton hammer 8-1 on aggregate in the UEFA Cup Third Round in 2008?
SK Brann

4) Everton were knocked out of the UEFA Cup in the First Round by which team in 2008?
Standard Liege

5) Everton qualified for the knockout stages of the 2009/10 Europa League by finishing second in the group stage, behind which team?
Benfica

6) Everton topped the table in their 2014/15 Europa League group by beating Wolfsburg by what score in the final group stage game?
4-1

7) Who knocked Everton out of the 2014/15 Europa League at the last 16 stage?
Dynamo Kyiv

8) Everton managed only one win during their Europa League 2017/18 campaign, beating which team 3-0 away from home?
Apollon Limassol

9) Which referee controversially ruled out a Duncan Ferguson goal to effectively end their hopes of beating Villarreal in the qualifying round of the Champions League in 2005?
Pierluigi Collina

10) What was the aggregate score line in that Champions League Qualifying Round tie?
Villarreal 4-2 Everton

Printed in Great Britain
by Amazon